The Website Success Accelerator Teaches..

– How To....

Get Ranked

The Art of Search Engine Optimisation and Getting Indexed Fast

By Charly Leetham

Published by Dreamstone Publishing 2012, 2013 and 2014

Look out for Other Books in

The Website Success Accelerator Teaches..

Series, coming soon

ISBN: 098737141X

ISBN13 :978-0-9873714-1-6

If you would like to provide feedback on this book please send it to info@digitalwordpress.com

What Readers Are Saying About This Book

"What a wonderful assistance this guide has been. I have read and implemented this guidance and found some fantastic results. I can highly recommend this book to anyone that need to 'get up and running' very quickly" - **Business Guru**

"Very clear and easy to follow instructions without the fluff! Awesome bonus links, tutorials and tool recommendations too - a must have for every website owner wanting to quickly learn about DIY search engine optimization! Looking forward to the series :)" - **KO**

DISCLAIMER

The contents of this manual reflect the author's views acquired through her experience on the topic under discussion.

The author and publisher disclaims any personal loss or liability caused by the utilization of any information presented herein. The author is not engaged in rendering any legal or professional advice. The services of a professional person are recommended if legal advice or assistance is needed.

While the sources mentioned herein are assumed to be reliable at the time of writing, the author and publisher, or their affiliates are not responsible for their activities.

From time to time, sources may terminate or move and prices may change without notice. Sources can only be confirmed reliable at the time of original publication of this manual.

This manual is a guide only and, as such, should be considered solely for basic information. Earnings or profits derived from participating in the following program are entirely generated by the ambitions, motivation, desires, and abilities of the individual reader.

No part of this manual may be altered, copied, or distributed, without prior written permission of the author or publisher.

All product names, logos, and trademarks are property of their respective owners who have not necessarily endorsed, sponsored, or approved this publication.

Text and images available over the internet and used in this manual may be subject to intellectual rights and may not be copied from this manual.

Table of Contents

Thank You For Buying This Book !

I hope that you enjoy it

If you do, please let others know by reviewing this book on Amazon.

How to Use This Book

This book is presented in Chapters, and Sections within Chapters. For each Chapter or Section, there may be Bonus Content that you can get from the links provided.

These pieces of Bonus content may be reports, videos or audios on the relevant topics, and allow you to receive much more information and detail, and understand it better, than just making this a huge book of boring text.

To find the Bonus Content, look for the Present Box icon –

Bonus Content:

Bonus Content will usually be presented grouped together at the end of the section it supports and relates to.

To view the Bonus Content, use the link and coupon code provided at the end of the Introduction to register, then just click on/touch the links provided, and you will be taken to the www.askcharlyleetham.com or the www.websitesuccessaccelerator.com website to view it.

Introduction

This guide has been written to aid small businesses and solopreneurs in understanding Search Engine Optimisation, how it can benefit your business and how you can achieve good Search Engine Optimisation results by using simple, easy to follow steps.

If you've done any research into getting your site indexed and onto Page 1 of Google, you'll know that the "Guru's" will have us believe that SEO is hard and that it takes forever to see your site indexed in the search engines, let alone on Page 1.

If you don't follow a certain formula, getting indexed, let alone on Page 1 of Google is an incredibly difficult task. However, from experience, I know that if you follow the techniques that I am going to share with you in this book, you will soon be indexed and have a high likelihood of being found on Page 1.

The techniques discussed in this book can be applied to any website.

However, many of the practical steps that I provide are for use with a Wordpress website.

I prefer to use Wordpress as a website platform, as it is easy to setup, configure and maintain. Additionally, there are a number of free plug-ins that you can use to aid in the optimisation of your website for search engines.

Bonus Content:

There are several video tutorials referenced in this book. To gain access to these tutorials visit:

http://websitesuccessaccelerator.com/get-ranked

and use coupon code: **kd0998**

Chapter 1 - What Is Search Engine Optimisation?

Search Engine Optimisation (SEO) is the process of setting your website up to ensure that it is listed in the Search Engine Result Pages (SERPs), for the topics that you want to be found for, and have those results listed on Pages 1 or 2, preferably.

When creating a website, particularly a selling or educational website, you want people to find your site when they search for a specific problem.

> For example, *a 15 year old girl may be searching for a way to reduce the acne that she is experiencing. You may have a great natural cure that is perfect for a young teen, and you want her to come your site to find that cure.*

By utilising correct SEO techniques, you will be able to ensure that, not only is your site listed on the Search Engines, but the page with that specific cure is also listed.

When we talk about your site being listed in the SERPs, we are referring to getting it listed in the organic (or natural) search engine results, not the paid results, and preferably on the first or second pages.

Looking at a Google Search Result Page, you'll notice that Paid Advertisements (Google Adwords) appear on the right hand side of the page and sometimes at the top of the page (the ones at the top of the page generally have a very pale yellow background behind them).

The organic results appear on the left hand side of the page.

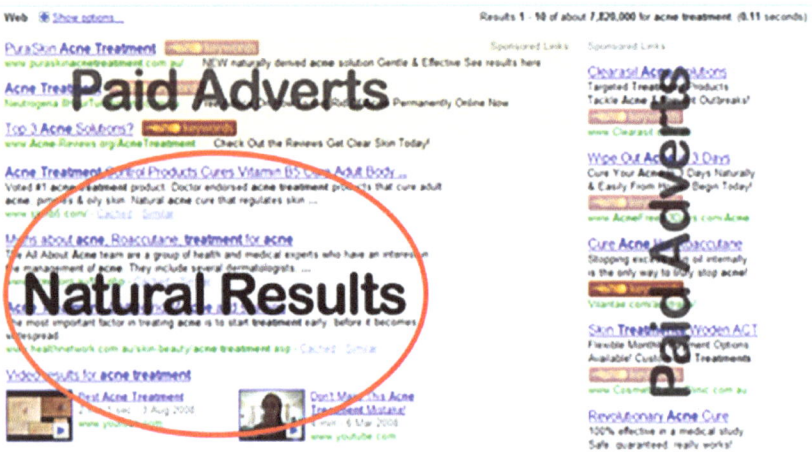

Figure 1 Google Search Engine Results Page

To boil the information right down, Search Engine Optimisation is the ability to get your site listed in the Search Engines, for the keywords or keyphrases you choose, preferably on page 1.

Why Search Engine Optimisation?

Whilst you could leave the indexing of your website to chance, or utilise other traffic generating techniques, like Social Media Marketing or Pay Per Click (PPC) advertising, spending the time to ensure that your site is optimised for the Search Engines is a worthwhile activity.

By optimizing your site for Search Engines, you are taking advantage of the free traffic that is generated through the Search Engines.

Market Research

Proper Search Engine Optimisation requires you to undertake keyword research, to find out what people are really searching for, how many searches are conducted and how much competition exists for that specific keyword.

From a business management perspective, this is a critical part of creating a new product or service, or targeting a new market – to know what your prospects are looking for and to see how you can deliver the results.

Keyword Research will help you target specific words and phrases, that you want the Search Engines to list you for, but it will also help you to decide whether there is really a market for the product or service that you are looking to sell or promote.

Getting Indexed

By following the basic Search Engine Optimisation steps, you will be able to get your site indexed (listed in the search engines) relatively quickly.

Even with the popularity of services like Twitter and Facebook, that will allow you to promote to an audience, many people still rely on the traditional web search services to find the information that they are looking for – and you want to make sure that you are found wherever your target audience is looking.

Cost Savings

Being found naturally in the SERPs is like having a FREE Yellow Pages advertisement. Once you've undertaken the basic SEO steps, and continue to use the process with new information you add to your site, you are literally getting free advertising.

If you do your SEO job well enough, you will also get your site listed near the top of the listing – with Yellow Pages advertisements and similar, you have to pay a premium for this.

Chapter 2 - Understanding the Search Engines

In order to gain visibility, and popularity, on the internet, you'll want a better understanding of how the search engines do what they do. In this section, I'm going to discuss some of the basics.

Algorithms

Algorithm is the technical term for a series of steps and rules for finding a solution to a problem. Algorithms involving computers are automated and proceed through a series of prearranged, logical steps in order to solve fundamental problems or common operational procedures.

It's a lot like baking a cake or servicing a car – you follow a predefined set of steps to achieve success.

The theory is that the search engines study your pages (literally read your pages in an electronic way) using certain criteria, such as the amount of links pointing back to your site, the location and frequency of keywords and how unique and relevant your content is, to determine where your site will rank in the SERP's.

Pagerank

Google assigns a numeric values (known as pagerank (PR)) to web pages based on certain criteria. The basic purpose of pagerank is to list web pages, from the most important to the least important, on the SERP's, when a keyword search occurs.

Pagerank is a link analysis algorithm, which means that if a website has a lot of links from other large websites that also rank well (otherwise known as authority sites) then the theory is that website will also be ranked highly.

PR is just one of the hundreds of algorithms that Google uses to rank web pages. Google even has a toolbar that you can install that has a smaller version of the PR algorithm that will display any given web page's PR of 0 – 10, 0 being obscure and 10 being a highly visible page.

PR can come in handy because it can give you some idea of the popularity of a page, which can give you some idea of whether you may want to link to, without doing in depth research.

Keep in mind that these values are adjusted depending on numerous reasons and using an algorithm based solely on Google's rules, which can change from time to time.

No one ever knows exactly what factors Google places importance on however, enough information has been passed along to know that, as well as backlinks, things like keywords and unique, relevant content all play an important role in how Google ranks your site.

The 3 Major Search Engines

When you are optimising your site for the search engines, it's best to concentrate your efforts on the ones that are going to bring you the most traffic.

For that reason, we focus on optimising our sites for Google because it is the number 1 Search Engine, with over 60% of users using Google to perform searches.

Yahoo comes in 2nd with 20% and MSN's BING rounding up 3rd with 10%.

Search Engine Share - April 2014

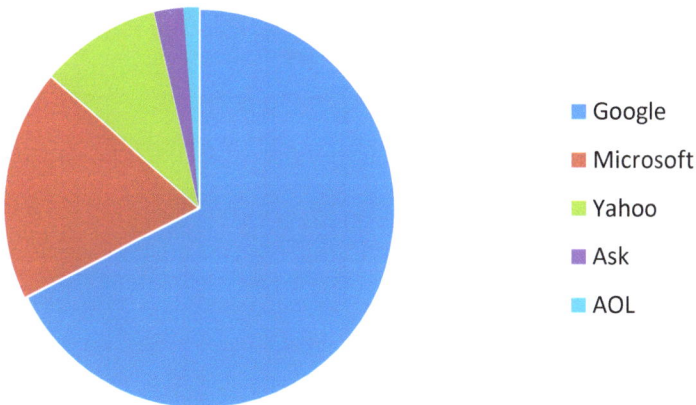

- Google
- Microsoft
- Yahoo
- Ask
- AOL

As a result, it is best to focus most of your SEO efforts on Google, since not only do they receive most of the traffic, but once you get indexed in their results, the others will catch on and you will start seeing traffic from them as well.

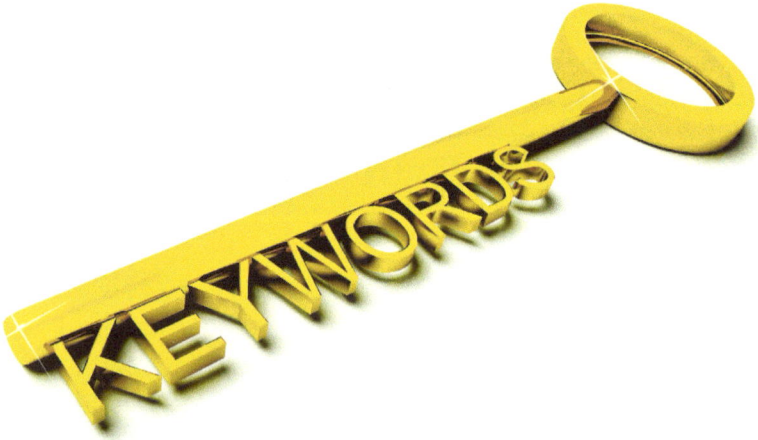

Chapter 3 - Before You Even Begin

Before you even begin creating your website – even before you register your domain name, you need to do your keyword research to ensure that you are targeting the best possible keywords for your chosen niche.

By choosing the right keywords, you will be able to minimise competition thus increasing the opportunity for your Search Engine listing to be found.

Keywords are KEY

Choosing the right keywords is not an easy task. You may think that you know exactly what your target keyword should be, but even the slightest variation – maybe making it plural – can cause significant differences in traffic to your site.

For example, using the keyword *Acne* will have a lot of competition (over 23 million searches at the time of writing).

Natural Acne Remedies will have considerably less (over 3 million at the time of writing)

Natural Acne Remedies for Young Teens will have even less (just over 39,000 at the time of writing).

As you can see, by becoming targeted with your keywords, you are focussing on a specific problem, and only being found by the people who are searching for a solution to that specific problem, not something related (eg natural acne cures for older people), and considerably reducing the amount of competition.

Definitely a Win-Win. Sometimes, targeted keywords like *Natural Acne Remedies For Young Teens* are also called long tail keywords.

NOTE: As a general rule, single keywords will be extremely competitive. Your goal with your keyword research is to find keywords with low competition and around 3,000 to 4,000 searches per month.

Researching Your Keywords

Free Tools

When conducting Keyword research, I recommend using Google's Adwords Keyword Planner (https://adwords.google.com/KeywordPlanner). There are many paid keyword analysis tools however, in most cases the Google tool is great. It is excellent and free to use, although to get access to the full range of its features you will need to sign up for an Adwords account but Don't Panic!

Basic Keyword Analysis

The first thing you want to do is to make a list of what you believe will be the main keywords for your site. Remember that keywords can be single words, or phrases. Don't worry about the fact that you are using broad keywords here... you're just using them to start your research and gain more information. Now that you have your basic keywords, go to Google's Adwords Keyword Planner (https://adwords.google.com/KeywordPlanner) and select *Search for new keyword and ad group ideas*

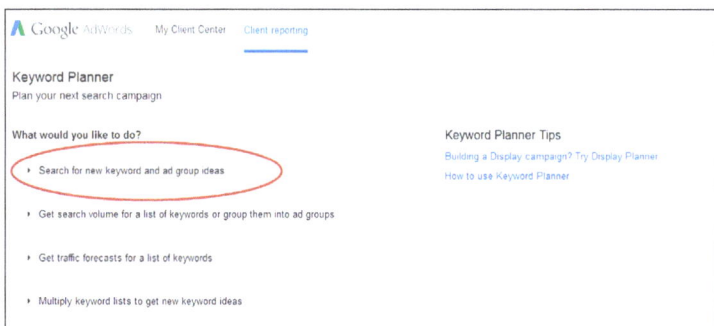

The following screen will be displayed:

What would you like to do?

▾ Search for new keyword and ad group ideas

Enter one or more of the following: 1

Your product or service

acne
natural acne remedy

Your landing page

www.example.com/page 2

Your product category

Enter or select a product category 3

Targeting ❓

All locations 4

English 5

Google 6

Negative keywords 7

Date range ❓

Show avg. monthly searches for: Last 12 months 8

Customize your search ❓

Keyword filters 9

Keyword options 10
Show broadly related ideas
Hide keywords in my account
Hide keywords in my plan

Keywords to include 11

Get ideas

Complete the boxes as follows:

1. Your Product or Service

This are the terms that you feel that people are searching for or which relate to your product or service. Enter 1 term per line

2. Your Landing Page

Enter the URL to a page on your website that relates to the product and / or service that you want to promote. The tool will scan the page and select keywords for you. This can be left blank.

3. Your Product Category

To refine the keyword search, you can select a product category that best relates to your product or service. This can be left blank.

Your product category

Enter or select a product category	
All Categories	
Apparel	≫
Arts & Entertainment	≫
Beauty & Personal Care	≫
Business & Industrial	≫
Computers & Consumer Electronics	≫
Dining & Nightlife	≫
Family & Community	≫
Finance	≫
Food & Groceries	≫
Health	≫
Hobbies & Leisure	≫
Home & Garden	≫
Internet & Telecom	≫
Jobs & Education	≫
Law & Government	≫
News, Media & Publications	≫
Occasions & Gifts	≫
Real Estate	≫
Retailers & General Merchandise	≫
Sports & Fitness	≫
Travel & Tourism	≫
Vehicles	≫

4. Locations

If your product or service is regionally based or geographically targeted, retrieving keywords for an international or global audience isn't the most appropriate approach. Use the locations setting to refine the details of your keyword search to best suit the locations where your product and service is sold.

5. Language

Select the Languages that you wish to target for your products and services. Hold the CTRL key down to select multiple languages.

6. Search networks to use

Select "Google" or "Google and search engines" to retrieve results from

7. Negative keywords

There are some keywords you will never want to include in your SEO strategy. These are the words that you would include in the box.

For example if our keyword is "Natural Acne Remedies for Teens", a search is likely to provide "Natural Acne Remedies for Adults". Adding Adults to that "exclude" field would stop this from happening.

8. Date Range

Refine the date range to return results for. The length of time you select is dependent on your product / service.

9. Keyword Filters

Average monthly searches 🔢

≥ ∨

Suggested bid 🔢

≥ ∨ A$

Ad impression share 🔢

≥ ∨

Competition

☐ High ☐ Medium ☐ Low

To determine appropriate terms to target for SEO, the Average monthly searches and Competition are the most appropriate to set.

The average monthly searches is the number of searches conducted for each term.

I would recommend looking at all results first and then incrementally refine the results when volumes are known.

Competition refers to the amount of paid advertising for a particular term.

I recommend that you look for keywords that have Medium to Low paid competition.

10. Keyword Options

Keyword options

OFF	Only show ideas closely related to my search terms
OFF	Show keywords in my account
OFF	Show keywords in my plan
OFF	Show adult ideas

Only show ideas closely related to my search terms will return synonyms or similar terms to your search terms.

Show keywords in my account and Show keywords in my plan should be off. These are for AdWords campaigns.

Show Adult Ideas applies if you are running an adult-oriented site.

11. Keywords to Include

Only include keywords containing the following terms:

To exclude keywords, add negative keywords using your targeting options.

If it is important that a specific keyword be included as part of your SEO strategy, add it to the include box in this section.

This will ensure that the term is always added to your keyword list.

When all the detail is entered, click the "Get Ideas" button and the results screen will be displayed.

Click on the *Keyword Ideas tab*

The goal here with your keyword research is to locate keywords with low competition, and a reasonable number of searches each month.

You will need to spend some time doing this research, and you may find that it gets a little frustrating – but it is well worth it in the long run.

It is a good idea to capture the results that you find for your keywords in a table or spreadsheet so that you can compare them later to make a decision about which ones to use.

Registering Your Domain Name

If you haven't already registered your domain name – use the keywords that you have chosen from your keyword research in your domain name.

For example, if you decide to target Natural Acne Remedies For Teens, then register something similar to

www.NaturalAcneRemediesForTeens.com, or perhaps choose

www.MyNaturalAcneRemediesForTeens.com, or

www.NaturalAcneRemediesForTeensToday.com

– each of these domains have your keywords.

By incorporating your keywords into your domain name, you are aiding your Search Engine Optimisation.

You can register domain names at

www.CheapDomainNamesToday.com.

When search engines begin the process of indexing your site, they also consider the length of time that your domain has been registered for – as this goes to show 'intent' for the site.

If you've registered your domain name for only 12 months (because you want to see how it will go), your site will not receive as high a ranking as another that has a domain registered for 2, 5 or 10 years.

I recommend registering your domain name for a minimum of 2 years.

There are some schools of thought that consider that you should register all the types of domains around your domain name.

For example, if you choose to register **www.MyAcneRemediesForTeens.com**, you should also choose the .org, .net and .info versions of that domain name.

The only real benefit of registering the different domain types is that you will be able to control your brand for that domain.

By that, I mean that if you register

www.MyAcneRemediesForTeens.com

and work hard to develop that brand, someone may register

www.MyAcneRemediesForTeens.net

and literally ride on your coat tails to receive traffic.

It is certainly something to consider in your planning process, but I have no recommendations to make on this point.

Chapter 4 - The Mechanics of SEO

Before we begin addressing how SEO works, it is prudent to point out that, unless you have high quality, unique content on your site, it is highly unlikely that your site will rank highly in the SERPs.

I address content within this section, but I really want to highlight the importance of content on your website to your Search Engine Optimisation endeavours.

There are really two parts to Search Engine Optimisation.

The first part is all of the things that you can do on your website to enhance your Search Engine Optimisation – we call this On-Page Optimisation.

The second part is all of the things you can do through the Internet, on other websites and the like. This is called Off-Page Optimisation.

On-Page Optimisation

Using Meta Tags

This is a simple technique that is often overlooked when setting up a website. Admittedly, the use of meta tags is not as powerful as it once was – but every little bit helps and it's worthwhile ensuring that you set these tags when you create each page (or post) on your site.

Title

The Title tag is not technically a Meta Tag, but it is very useful. This tag tells the search engine 'bots (spiders) what the page is about and sets the details in the bar at the top of your browser.

By setting the 'title' of your browser, you are letting your visitor know what they can expect on the page they are visiting. This is important as it sets the readers perception and prepares them for the information presented.

The TITLE tag is often used when listing your site or page in the SERPs:

Social Media Shortcuts - Do They Exist? | Ask Charly Leetham
The biggest challenge that most business people have is just how to use ...
askcharlyleetham.com/blog/social.../social-media-shortcuts-do-they-exist

1. Here are some simple guidelines for setting a great Title for each of your pages, and posts, on your websites:

2. Create a different title for each page or post on your site – this will ensure that each page or post is seen as a separate entity by the Search Engines

3. Make your title tag human readable, and use your keyword for that page. Some would advise that you place only keywords separated by commas or dashes – this is not recommended as it really looks like you are trying too hard – and it will not encourage searchers to click through on your listing. **Remember that the title is seen by your visitors, so make it readable by your visitors**.

4. Try to limit your Title to 70 characters - as that's all that most of the Search Engines will use when listing your site.

5. Use a separator to separate phrases. Eg. *Natural Acne Remedies |Acne Remedy For Young Teens*

6. Target longer keyphrases if possible. Eg. *Natural Acne Remedies | Remove Acne In 10 Days For Young Teens*

7. Target buyer intent wherever possible. For someone looking to buy an acne remedy, you may try a title like *Acne Remedies |Buy Natural Acne Remedy For Young Teens*

Meta Description

The Meta Description is the text that provides the 'excerpt' of what readers will find on the page. Whilst it isn't used in the ranking of a site, it is important to the overall user experience of the site. And some newer WordPress themes (usually magazine style themes)actually display it as party of the post thumbnail.

When writing your Meta Description, keep in mind the following tips:

1. Write the description in 160 characters or less

2. Include information in the description that is not contained within the title. I like to include a gracious 'Call To Action' in my descriptions, let people know what they will get by clicking through.

3. Use your keyword for that page in your description.

4. Make the description human readable. As with the Title, some will advise you to only use your keywords – consider how your description will look and read to people who are searching for what you are offering.

Keywords

This is the tag that lists the keywords that relate to your page.

Due to the high level of abuse that has been exercised with this tag, most Search Engines do not even look at this tag anymore.

I will, in general, enter my keywords for each page in this tag however, I do not expect it to have any impact on my search engine listings or rankings.

Typically, I will choose up to 5 keywords that relate to my page and set my meta keywords accordingly.

Creating the META tags on your pages

```
<HTML>
<HEAD>
<meta http-equiv=pragma content=no-cache>
<meta http-equiv=cache-control content=no-cache>
<meta http-equiv=expires content=0>
<meta content="work from home, affiliate marketing, niche products, free, private label rights, master resell rights, plr, mrr"
name=Keywords>
<meta content="Make Money from Home using Niche Products and Affiliate Marketing" name=Description>
<TITLE>Make Money working From Home</TITLE>
<?php
```

If you have a static html website, these tags are set in the actual HTML codes of the page.

On a Wordpress installation, setting the meta tags is somewhat easier.

The WordPress SEO plug-in :

http://wordpress.org/extend/plugins/wordpress-seo/

allows you to set the details specifically for each page or post.

Bonus Content:

For a Video Tutorial on installing and using All In One SEO Pack for your WordPress Blog go to:

http://websitesuccessaccelerator.com/1412/setting-up-wordpress-seo/go

Content

This is the most important part of your On-Page Search Engine Optimisation. The meta tags discussed above will provide you with a small advantage when being indexed however, nothing (and I repeat nothing) beats good content and this content really needs to be unique to your site.

"Content Is King" – whatever else you read or hear about getting your site indexed or getting it to Page 1 of Google, remember that this saying is as true today, as it ever has been.

In order to better serve your visitors, as well as the search engines, your site will require lots of relevant, unique content. For the purposes of SEO, relevant content simply means that it corresponds to the informational demands of the visitors that your site is targeting.

Unique Content

When the term unique content is used, it isn't referring to information that hasn't been shared anywhere else (although that would be GREAT!).

It is referring to the fact that when you share your information with your readers, it shouldn't be a direct copy and paste from another website (this raises copyright issues too), a reproduction of a Private Label Rights (PLR) article or other similar practices.

Your content needs to be written in a unique manner.

Contrary to some of the information you read about being 'delisted' if you don't use Unique Content, the main disadvantage is that you will never receive the credit for the content and thus never receiving the ranking for your site.

Using Your Keywords

When you write your page or post, it is incredibly important to decide what Keywords relate to that page. In general, you should target 1 keyword per page or post and use that phrase 'sparingly' throughout your content. If you use your keyword too many times, this could be considered as 'Keyword Stuffing' and your site 'delisted'.

A good rule of thumb is to use your keyword approximately 1 time per 100 words. This means that if your page is 300 words long, you should have used your keyword 3 times.

By making use of the formatting tools, like Bold, Underline and Italics, you can also indicate to the Search Engine Spiders that certain words or phrases are more important than others.

Make your content count – after all, the job of the search engines is to deliver relevant content to their customers. You can help them do their job better by ensuring that you have high quality, relevant content on your site.

Add new content regularly

Once you have your website setup, don't let it stagnate - add fresh content on a regular basis. Remember, it is the job of the Search Engines to deliver highly relevant search results to their customers and, if you aren't adding new content, your site relevancy will start to reduce.

An added bonus of adding new content regularly is that the Search Engines will continue to index your site.

You can add content regularly by adding new pages to your websites, or you can create a blog and add articles about your product or service, the challenges experienced by your target audience, the remedies you've found etc etc. The thing is to make the content informative enough so that the Search Engines will continue to visit and index your site.

If you have a static website, adding a blog on your website domain is a great idea and relatively easy to accomplish. That way, you can blog about your products and services and link back to the pages on your website that relate to your article.

How often you should add content is really up to you however, I recommend that you add content no less frequently than once every two weeks. Preferably, adding content once a week will yield far more benefit to you.

For a step by step guide on how you can set up a Wordpress Blog on your own hosting, visit Get Your Blog Online Today (http://askcharlyleetham.com/blog/products-services/get-your-blog-online-today).

Page Names or Permalinks

Ensuring that the way you name your page also supports your keywords aids in your Search Engine Optimisation efforts. For example if you have a page that is about facial masks that helped clean a young teenagers skin, you would name that page – acnefacialmasksforteens.html if you were running a static website.

When using Wordpress as your Content Management System, you can set your permalink structure to use the Headline (or Title) of your page or post to form the 'url'. To set the permalink structure of your Wordpress installation to use the Headline of your post or page, go to the Permalinks section under Settings in your Admin Console:

⚙ Permalink Settings

By default WordPress uses web URLs which have question marks and lots of numbers in them, howev ability to create a custom URL structure for your permalinks and archives. This can improve the aesthet compatibility of your links. A number of tags are available, and here are some examples to get you sta

Common settings

○ Default	http://theipodmovieclub.com/?p=123
○ Day and name	http://theipodmovieclub.com/2009/11/14/sample-post/
○ Month and name	http://theipodmovieclub.com/2009/11/sample-post/
○ Numeric	http://theipodmovieclub.com/archives/123
◉ Custom Structure	/%post_id%/%postname%

When you change the permalinks to a 'custom structure' set it to:

/%post_id%/%postname%

The %post_id% will add the unique numerical identifier for the post page to the URL. Whilst this is not the 'optimum' for search engine optimisation, it allows Wordpress to find the post being referenced far more quickly in the database.

If this setting is omitted, the retrieval of the data for the requested page can take a long time (and make the people reading your website unhappy!). It is a trade off between the load time of the page, and the Search Engine Optimisation of the post.

The %postname% variable will utilise the Headline that you set for the page or the post.

Note: If you have an existing Wordpress installation, that is already indexed – DO NOT change your permalink structure. It will cause all sorts of issues with your search engine indexing and links to your site.

Images

A good picture or photo on a page can really aid in improving your visitor's experience and increase their interaction on your site. Unfortunately, the Search Engine spiders don't 'read' images like they do text. An image looks like a big blank space on the page to a Search Engine spider, and this is not exactly a great thing. However, there is an answer!

When inserting an image onto a page, you should make use of the ALT text to describe in words what an image is about. Here are some tips to consider when adding an Image and ALT Text

1. Only apply the following tips if your image is related to the keyword. If the image is not related to the keyword, then name your image with a number instead of a name. E.g if the image is a Subscribe Now button, name the image 2.jpg or 2.gif. This will indicate to the Search Engine Spiders that the image is not to be considered in the indexing process.

2. Use your targeted keyword for the page in the ALT text for the image. E.g If the keyword for the page is *Natural Acne Remedy For Young Teens*, and your image is a picture is of a teenage girl with acne (or clear skin) - set the ALT Text to *Natural Acne Remedy For Young Teens*

3. Give the image a filename that is related to your keyword. E.g My image name would be naturalacneremedyforyoungteens.gif or similar.

Admin Pages

There are certain pages that the search engine spiders are looking for that you really must include on your website.

The search engine providers understand that these pages are important to the overall website and in order for your website to rank high, these pages need to exist.

CONTACT US

Your website visitors must know how to contact you. You should keep this page simple – provide email addresses, phone numbers and support information.

PRIVACY POLICY

This is imperative to show the search engines that you are complying with the SPAM laws.

Your Privacy Policy indicates to your visitors that you take their privacy seriously and will not share their information with any other parties.

If you need to find a Privacy Policy, I've found www.FreeNetLaw.com to be a good site for generic templates.

Off Page Optimisation

There are many 'bits' to the puzzle that form Off Page Optimisation. However, overall it boils down to two things: Domain Age and relevant, **high quality links** back to your site.

Domain Age

Domain age is an important part of off page SEO. The older your domain and the longer that it has been registered, the better, as the search engines will assume that your site is an authority site and rank it accordingly. There really isn't much you can do here, but have patience.

Back Links

Back Links are simply links from other sites back to your site. When someone creates a post on their site and puts a link to your site in that post, that is classed as a backlink.

Google places a relatively high level of importance on the links to your site – they are like a vote of popularity but, due to a high level of abuse by site owners, the importance of links to your site has lessened somewhat.

However, the effectiveness of back links should not be underestimated. Back links can have a dual purpose – Getting Indexed and Improving Rankings in the Search Engines.

Getting Indexed

The first purpose is that, when used appropriately, backlinks can actually help your site be indexed more quickly. When you first put your site online, the Search Engines do not know about it and we have to 'somehow' tell the search engines that your site exists.

Improving Rankings

A backlink is just like a 'popularity vote'. Essentially, the more backlinks you have to your site – the more popular it is, and the Search Engines take this into consideration. However, not all backlinks are considered equal – and you should be focussed on getting links back from sites within your niche, or related to your content. When building links to your site – ensure that you are building quality links.

Things To Avoid

I strongly recommend that you DO NOT use the 'submit to search engine' functions that abound – not even the paid services. My research indicates that Search Engines consider that you are 'trying too hard' to get listed and you MAY be penalised for using these services.

Do NOT use Free For All (FFA) linking schemes – it is considered a form of spamming. A 'Free For All' link is a website where you can submit your website url and have that submitted to 100s of other sites. Using these types of schemes are detrimental to your Search Engine Optimisation success.

Things To Do

Ping Your Site

This is a simple process that announces to the many different authority type sites, that your website has been updated. You can do this manually by using www.pingomatic.com. Enter your site details, select "check all" and click 'send pings' every time you update or create a new page.

For Wordpress websites, you can automate this process by utilising the "update services" setting under wp-admin ->settings.

Bonus Content:

A list of the directories that I configure cbNet Ping Optimizer with is provided on the following link:

http://askcharlyleetham.com/specials/gr-cbfull/pingdirs/login

All you need to do is cut and paste the list into the configuration panel for cbNet Ping Optimizer.

Create a Sitemap and submit it to the Search Engines

A sitemap can be created in XML format, which is readable by computers (and search engines).

The sitemap is literally the electronic representation of your website and creating it and allowing the search engines access to it, you are 'making it easy' for them to index your site.

For static websites or sites that don't automatically create an XML sitemap, you can create your sitemap using an online tool like www.xml-sitemaps.com.

For Wordpress websites, I recommend the use of the WordPress SEO Plugin:

http://wordpress.org/extend/plugins/wordpress-seo/

to automate the creation and update of your XML sitemap.

To submit your sitemap to Google, you will need to sign up to Google Webmaster Tools :

https://www.google.com/webmasters/tools/home?hl=en

and follow the prompts to add a site, and submit a sitemap for inclusion.

Bonus Content:

Visit :

http://websitesuccessaccelerator.com/1416/xml-sitemaps-and-more/go

for videos demonstrating

1. Installing the Google XML Sitemaps plug-in for WordPress.

2. Creating an xml sitemap manually

3. Signing up for Google Webmaster Tools

4. Adding a site to Google Webmaster Tools and verifying your site

5. Submitting a sitemap to Google Webmaster Tools

6. Signing up for Yahoo

7. Notifying Yahoo automatically when new content is added

Building Links

Getting high quality, relevant links to your site is an important, but possibly time consuming, task. However, overall it is worth the effort.

By gaining links to your site, you are not only helping the search engines to find your site (getting indexed) you are essentially telling the search engines how popular your site is.

Getting Your Site Indexed

When you generate links from other sites, you are also increasing the possibility of your site being indexed.

This happens because when a spider indexes the site that your link appears on, if the DoFollow tag is set, the spider will literally follow the link to your site and then indexes your site.

Let's discuss how you can generate backlinks from other websites.

Blog and Forum Commenting

One of the simplest methods to generate backlinks from other websites, is to become involved in the discussion. To become involved in the discussion, sometimes all you need to do is add a comment.

This works particularly well on blogs and to a limited degree on Forums.

If you choose a blog or a forum that has the DoFollow tag set, and add your website address – your site will be indexed.

There are a few things to consider when embarking on this strategy:

1. Make sure that you are adding to the discussion. DO NOT add comments like "Great Post, Thanks For Sharing" – these comments are most likely going to be SPAMMED.

2. When adding your website url, use your Keywords as the anchor text... that is, the text that shows as the clickable link, should contain your keywords. E.g If your keyword is Acne Remedy For Young Teens, then your link should be Acne Remedy For Young Teens.

How to Comment on Blogs

To comment on a Blog, and have your Keywords show up as your link, you should enter your Keywords in the name field on the comment form and your website in the Website field (see the image below).

When the comment is added, the blog will automatically link the website to your name.

When you add your comment, ensure that it adds to the conversation and shares your experiences.

Of course, you should use your keywords wherever possible in the comment – but not more than once every 100 words.

Be aware though – some blog owners may not appreciate you linking your Keywords through your name, they may consider that as Spam and will delete the comment.

Exercise caution when implementing this technique and try not to look spammy!

Comment adds to the conversation

Name (required)

Acne Remedy For Young Teens

Email Address (required)

youremail@email.com

Website

http://acneremedyforyoungteens.com

Speak your mind

This is a tip! I suffered with acne when I was a teenager and I can say that I used exactly this method and it helped clear up my acne very quickly. I also found that using a Tea Tree oil cleanser was great as well.

Keep up the great work!

Sara

Submit Comment

Discussions On Forums

Forums are also a great place to add to the conversation, gain information for yourself and credential yourself as an expert in the area.

Forums can however, be time consuming and participation shouldn't be taken lightly. Be prepared to dedicate regular time each week to this strategy.

To participate in a forum, you should get involved in the conversations that are occurring, add your thoughts and advise and ask questions yourself.

Most forums will allow you to add a signature to your profile which is automatically added to the posts you create on a forum.

When you create your signature, you should use your targeted keywords in your signature. So using our Acne Remedies For Young Teens, your forum signature may be:

> Your Name
>
> Natural Acne Remedies For Young Teens

Within a forum post, you may use:

> I've found one of the best natural acne remedies for young teens to be….

Note: Ensure that you review the Terms Of Service for the forum that you participate in, before adding your signature to your profile. Often, it is best to participate in the forum for a short while before adding your signature, that way you won't appear to only be interested in marketing!

Bookmarking

Social Bookmarking, or Bookmarking, is the process of adding your site, page or post to an online bookmarking service to share with your community.

Much like saving a bookmark on our browser, you can save a link to a favourite website on specialised 'bookmarking websites' – and it doesn't have to be just your website, you can share other sites of interest with your community.

Bookmarking works to get your site indexed and ranking higher in the SERPs because most Social Bookmarking sites are considered 'authority sites' by the Search Engines.

Be aware though, that some bookmarking sites seem to work better than others, and this can depend on the niche that you are targeting.

It is worthwhile spending a bit of time looking at some of the sites to see if they have a particular 'flavour' to what is added.

Care should be taken not to 'abuse' bookmarking.

Some simple guidelines to follow to ensure that you don't abuse bookmarking include:

- Not bookmarking on the same day of the week; and

- Bookmarking other sites of interest other than your own (even if they aren't in your niche);

There are several bookmarking sites on the internet today, some are more appropriate for specific niches than others. Some of the most popular bookmarking sites (at the time of publication) are:

- Digg
- Fark
- del.icio.us
- StumbleUpon
- Faves
- Mixx
- Technorati
- Yahoo Buzz
- Newsvine
- Kaboodle
- Reddit
- Slashdot
- Propeller

This is by no means an exhaustive list – there are many more bookmarking sites that you can use.

I recommend (and use) the OnlyWire bookmarking service (http://onlywire.com/).

When you create and setup an Onlywire account, you can automatically submit your bookmarks to a number of bookmarking sites.

It takes some time to setup an OnlyWire account, but that time will save you more time than that every time you use it.

When you create a new page, or new post on your site – bookmark it with OnlyWire to add links to your site and let people know what you are doing.

Social Networking Sites: Facebook, Twitter, Linked In and More....

You can share your new pages and posts on sites and services like Facebook, Twitter and Linked In.

I don't recommend that you blast these sites with your links ALL THE TIME, but certainly share your updates.

A great way to automate this process is to use Hootsuite.

Hootsuite allows you to take an RSS Feed and 'feed' to your Twitter, Facebook, Linked In, and Google Plus profiles.

By feeding your content to your social networks, you will create links that carry a high level of Authority with Google and raising your communities awareness of your content.

Article Marketing

Article Marketing is possibly the most effective method to generate links to your site – but the link building is a slow process.

There are two more benefits to Article Marketing – the first one being that your site will be indexed through your articles and the second reason being that you can credential yourself as an Expert in your field through your articles.

Content Is The Key

Great content is the key to having your articles read, and republished on other sites. An ideal article is between 400 and 750 words in length, although many article directories and sites will use articles that are as short as 200 words.

The article should be informative and educational – not salesy.

The idea is to credential yourself as an expert and provide value to the readers. Articles that discuss a product or service should compare 2 to 3 similar products and services to provide a basis for the opinion.

You should use your keywords throughout your article but **no more than twice every 100 words** BUT make sure that the article reads naturally.

Read your article aloud to ensure that it reads correctly.

Keep links to a minimum within the article body.

Preferably, don't use links at all within the body as this can appear to be too salesy and many people won't reprint these types of articles. Make use of the Author resource box to do your linking.

Getting the Back Link

To gain that all important backlink and drive traffic to your website, a well crafted Author Resource Box is essential.The author resource box is displayed at the bottom of the article and will look something like:

About The Author:

Your Name is a natural therapist who specialises in natural acne remedies. Her website at http://www.mywebsite.com offers effective advice on acne remedies for young teens.

Receive a free guide on natural acne remedies by sending a blank email to:
mailto: acneremedies@myautoresponder.com
 or at http://www.mywebsite.com

Your Author Resource Box is added to the bottom of each and every one of your articles when published. It's important that you include your selected keywords in your resource box but don't overuse the keywords – again, use your keywords once or twice in every 100 words.

You gain a backlink each time your article is republished on someone else's site – which aids in improving the ranking for your site.

Article Directories To Submit To

- Ezine Articles (http://ezinearticles.com/)
- Go Articles (http://goarticles.com/)
- Associated Content

  (http://askcharlyleetham.com/blog/associatedcontent)
- Qondio

  (see - http://askcharlyleetham.com/blog/qondio)

You can also submit your article automatically to 100's of directories and blogs, through Unique Article Wizard, (see - http://askcharlyleetham.com/blog/uaw) which is a paid service.

Content Websites

A content website allows you to create 1 page websites on their platform to share your information.

The benefit of these sites is that you can create 'satellite' pages that promote your product, service / brand and link back to your site.

Content sites are considered authority sites with the Search Engines and linking from these sites aids in the ranking of a website in the SERPs.

Content sites include Hubpages

(see - http://askcharlyleetham.com/blog/hubpages).

Caution should be exercised when adding content to these sites to ensure that you comply with the Terms of Service for these sites and that you don't appear 'spammy' with your content.

Here are some tips for using these sites appropriately to add content, remain within the Terms Of Service, and deliver value to your readers:

1. Add good content to your page on these sites. Just like your articles, ensure that the content is informational and educational and doesn't sell overtly.

2. Break your content into smaller, readable modules – this makes it easier for the visitors to read your content and take action.

3. Use your keywords in your content, but not more than once or twice ever 100 words, and link back to your site using your keywords (just like in your Author Resource Box).

4. When using Hubpages, you MUST use unique content. Hubpages won't publish duplicate content.

How Does Bookmarking, Articles and Content Sites Help You Get Indexed?

When you first 'get your site online', the search engines won't know about your site. In fact, they won't even know **to look for** your site to index it.

Whilst each of the search engines have a 'submission process', it is highly recommended that you don't use these services. An unconfirmed rumour that I have heard is that the Search Engines consider you are trying too hard if you use the submission process.

When you submit an article to a site like Ezine Articles, Bookmark your page or create a content page, you automatically gain a DoFollow link from a site that the Search Engines consider to be an Authority Site.

This is a great thing – firstly, because the site is considered to be an Authority Site, your article will be 'seen' sooner by the Search Engines and secondly, because the site uses DoFollow links, the Search Engine spiders will literally follow the links in your author resource box and index your site as well.

When first listing your website, it is not unusual to see your Articles, Bookmarking or Content Page ranking more highly than your website.

However once your site is indexed, as long as you are adding new, quality content, you will see that your site will soon rank higher than most of the sites linking back to it.

Submit Your Site To RSS Directories

If you have a site that has a RSS Feed, you can submit the site to RSS Directories for additional exposure. Your RSS feed is generally found by right clicking on the RSS Feed icon on the webpage and choosing Save Link As or Save Target As:

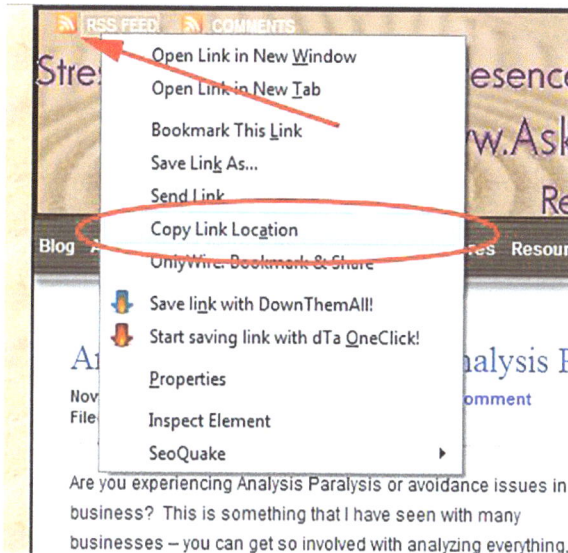

If you don't have a RSS Icon on your site, if you are running a WordPress based site, you can try using:

http://yourwebsite.com/?feed=rss -- If WordPress is installed in the Root Folder.

You will know that the link is correct if you receive a page that looks similar to:

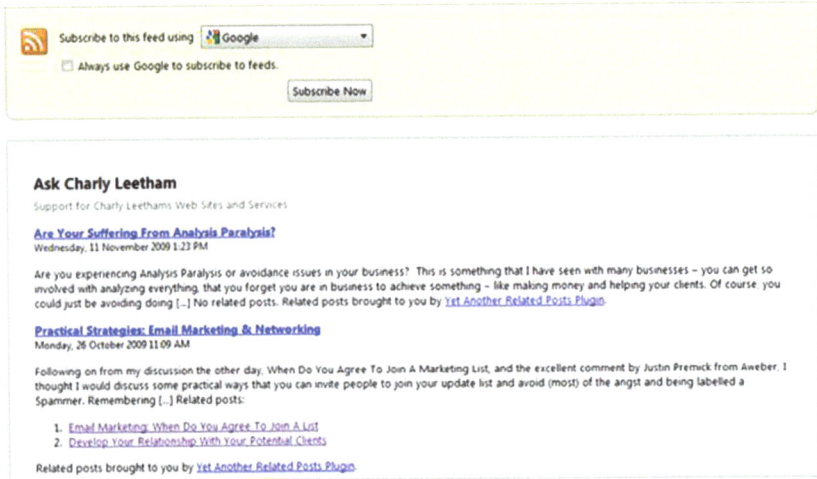

Once you have the RSS Feed URL, submit the feeds to www.feedage.com and www.feedest.com:

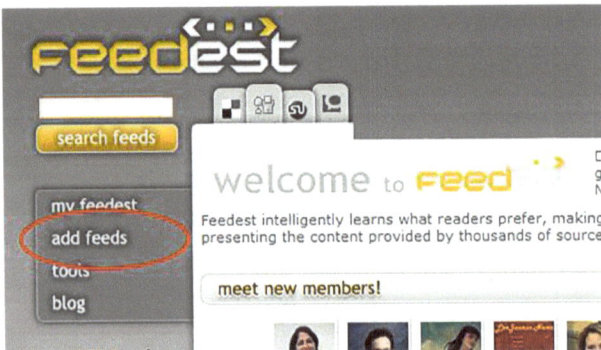

Chapter 5 - Setup Google Analytics

Testing and tracking is incredibly important to determine :

- which techniques are working,
- which sites are most effective for your efforts,
- where your visitors are coming from,
- what they are viewing and
- what keywords they used to access your content.

Google Analytics is wonderful for helping you to determine this information.

You will need a Google account for your Google Analytics.

You can use an existing account, or you can set up a separate account for your website.

The next few pages will take you through the process of setting up Google Analytics for your webaite.

Once you have your Google account then go to:

https://www.google.com/analytics/

and then click on the link in the top right hand corner that says "Access Google Analytics".

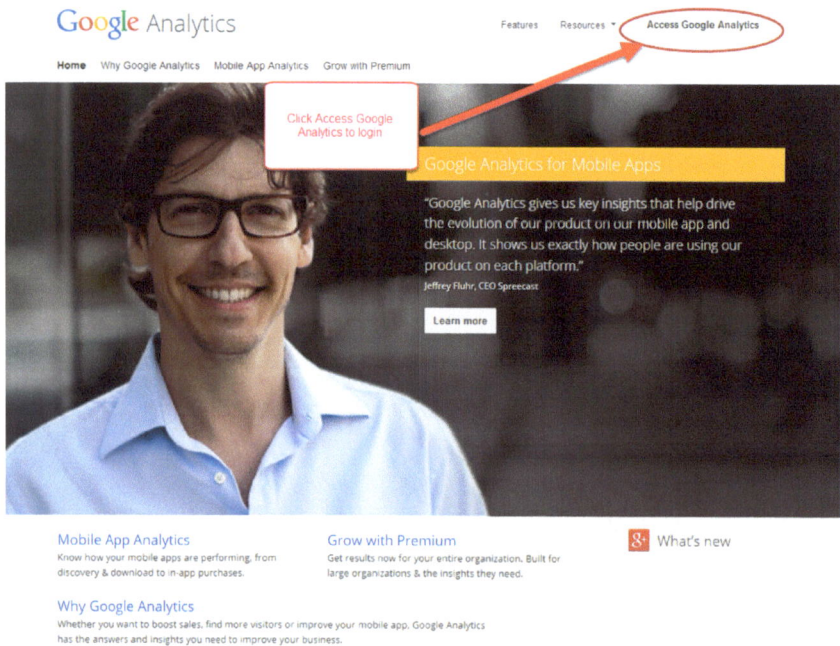

Login using your Google account.

You will then be prompted to sign up for the Analytics program and then enter your websites URL and other information.

Follow the directions and enter all of your information as required, agree to the terms of service and click on the "Create New Account" button.

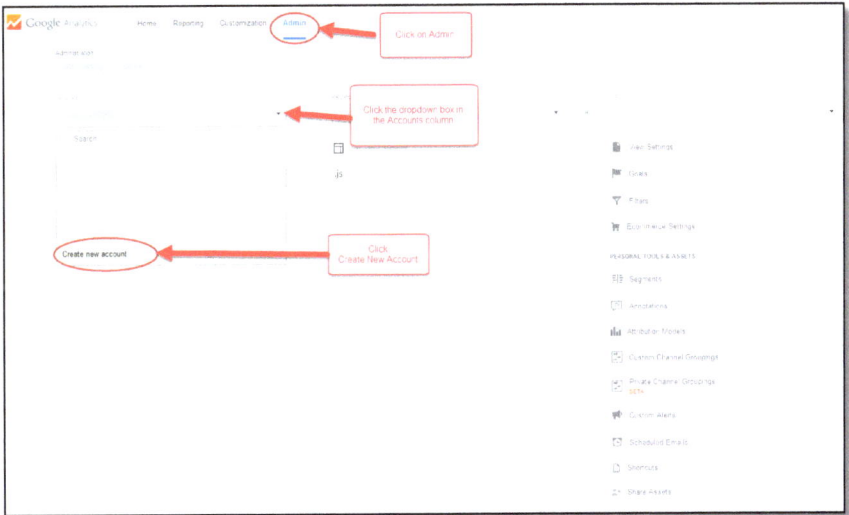

Follow the directions and enter all of your information as required,

New Account

What would you like to track?

Website   Mobile app

Tracking Method

This property works using Universal Analytics. Click *Get Tracking ID* and implement the Universal Analytics tracking code snippet to complete your set up.

Setting up your account

Account Name required
Accounts are the top-most level of organization and contain one or more tracking IDs.

My New Account Name   **1**

Setting up your property

Website Name required

My New Website   **2**

Website URL required

http:// ▾   Example: http://www.mywebsite.com   **3**

Industry Category

Select One ▾   **4**

Reporting Time Zone

United States ▾   (GMT-08:00) Pacific Time ▾   **5**

Data Sharing Settings

Fill in the form as follows:

1. Account Name

This is the name that you want to appear in the Accounts listing on Google Analytics.

2. Website Name

This is the name of the website that you want to monitor.

Make it informative so that there is no confusion if you have multiple websites.

3. Website URL

The url of the website you wish to monitor

4. Industry Category

Choose the category that best suits your product / service

5. Reporting Time Zone

Setting this will determine the times the analytics reports are provided in.

Once you have filled these in, move on to the data sharing settings.

Data Sharing Settings

Data that is collected, processed, and stored in your Google Analytics account ("Google Analytics data") is secure and kept confidential. Google Analytics data is used to provide and improve service, to perform system critical operations, and in rare exceptions for legal reasons as described in our privacy policy.

The data sharing options give you more control over sharing your Google Analytics data. Learn more.

✓ With other Google products only   [1]

Enable enhanced ad features, and an improved experience with AdWords, AdSense and other Google products by sharing your website's Google Analytics data with other Google services, and develop better Google services by sharing non-personal data. Only Google services (no third parties) will be able to access your data. Show example

✓ Anonymously with Google and others   [2]

Enable benchmarking by sharing your website data in an anonymous form. Google will remove all identifiable information about your website, combine the data with other anonymous sites in comparable industries and report aggregate trends in the benchmarking service. Show example

✓ Technical Support   [3]

Let Google technical support representatives access your Google Analytics data and account when necessary to provide service and find solutions to technical issues.

✓ Account specialists   [4]

Give Google marketing specialists and your Google sales specialists access to your Google Analytics data and account so they can find ways to improve your configuration and analysis, and share optimization tips with you. If you don't have dedicated sales specialists, give this access to authorized Google representatives.

Learn how Google Analytics safeguards your data.

Get Tracking ID   Cancel

1. Share with other Google Products Only

This should be checked. It allows the analytics data to be shared with AdWords and other google products for better integration and reporting.

2. Anonymously with Google and others

The data collected from your account will be used to provide aggregate market information, trends etc

3. Technical Support

Allow Google Tech Support access to your analytics data to provide assistance when needed

4. Account specialists

If you are seeking advice from Google on how to improve marketing campaigns etc, this should be ticked.

Now click on the "Get Tracking ID" button.

Next, you will be asked to agree to the terms of service.

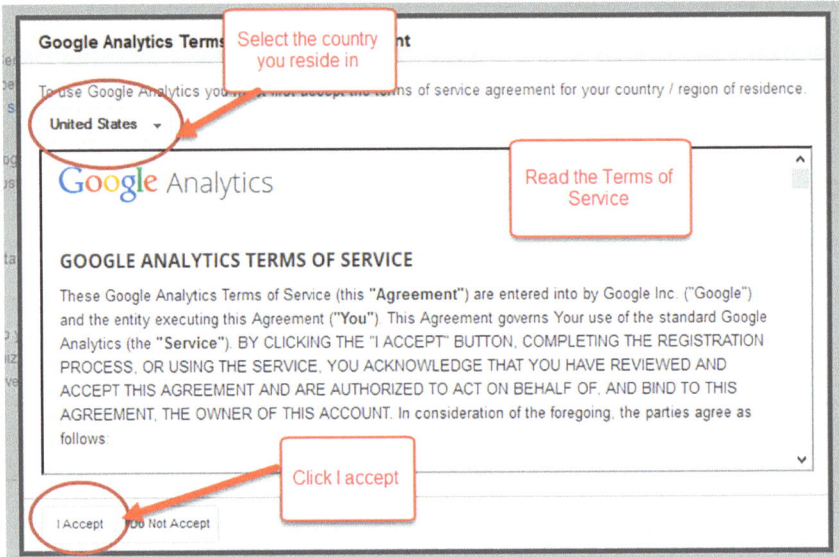

1. Select the country you reside in from the dropdown box on the top left

2. Read the Terms of Service

3. Click I Accept on the bottom left.

Once you do that, you will have your tracking code on the screen in front of you. Choose which format you want (it's best to choose "New Tracking Code"), select and copy the code.

On static websites, this code goes on the bottom of every web page that you want to track. In your pages HTML code, enter this code immediately before the </body> tag and generally, within 24 hours after you install the code, you should start seeing activity on your account.

If you are running a Wordpress website, adding Google Analytics is a lot easier and you can gain access to the statistics from your wp-admin dashboard. I recommend the use of any theme functionality that will allow the inclusion of the code or the Google Analyticor Plug-In (https://wordpress.org/plugins/google-analyticator/) to track your analytics and WordPress Analytics 360 Plug-In (https://wordpress.org/plugins/analytics360/) to view your statistics in your wp-admin Dashboard.

Once that is done, all that is left to do is analyse, test and tweak your pages to constantly increase your websites visibility, traffic and conversions.

Bonus Content:

Go to :

http://websitesuccessaccelerator.com/1402/creating-your-google-analytics-account/go

To view videos on how to:

1. Set up your Google Analytics account;
2. Install and setup the Google Analyticor and
3. Install and setup the Wordpress Google Analytics Reports plug-ins on your Wordpress Website.

In Summary

The process of getting your site indexed and ranking well in the SERP's is really a case of following a process, and ensuring that you are delivering quality content to your readers or site visitors.

To get your site indexed and ranking in the SERP's, the steps are simple but require attention to achieve correctly. Here they are, in order:

1. Conduct keyword research and target keywords that have a reasonably high search volume and lower competition

2. Register a domain name that uses your keywords

3. Create high quality, unique content on a regular basis for your site. Use your chosen keywords, in that content, no more than once or twice every 100 words.

4. Ensure that the Title, Meta Description and Meta Keywords fields are configured on each of your pages – using your targeted keywords from that page

5. Name your pages using your keywords

6. Name your images, and set the ALT text for your image, to correspond to your keywords, as long as that image relates to your keywords. If your image does not relate to your keywords, name the image with a number.

7. Bookmark your webpage using bookmarking sites

8. Comment on other Blogs or Forums in your niche, adding to the conversation and use your Keywords as the Anchor text.

   Where possible, find DoFollow blogs to comment on, but it's more important to add to the discussion on relevant and current blogs.

9. Write Articles, create an effective Author Resource Box that incorporates a link to your site using your keywords, and submit informative and useful articles to article directories.

10. Feed your new content to Social Networks like Twitter, Facebook and Linked In to gain backlinks and increase exposure.

11. Most importantly, keep writing and adding great content to your website so that the Search Engines can index your site regularly.

Other Great Resources

In my business, I apply SEO techniques every day, to my own websites, and those of my clients.

Over the years, I have learned about SEO through reading a lot of information and trying out different things, continuously keeping up to date with the regular changes in search engine algorithms and policies.

The one thing that I have found is that there are tried and true methods that work, time and time again, and that, whilst new techniques are created from time to time, it is often best to approach these techniques with caution and seek as many opinions as possible before implementing them on your website.

Throughout this book I have shared a number of resources that I use and recommend.

Many of the resources are free and a few are paid. In some cases I do receive a referral fee for any sales that I refer using those links.

These resources are ones that I recommend for anyone who wants to do their own SEO and learn more about SEO

Keyword Analysis

- Google's Adwords Keyword Analysis tool

  (https://adwords.google.com/select/KeywordToolExternal)

Domain Registrations

- www.CheapDomainNamesToday.com – register your domain names

Getting Indexed

- www.pingomatic.com

- www.xml-sitemaps.com

- Google Webmaster Tools

- WordPress SEO Plugin

  (http://wordpress.org/extend/plugins/wordpress-seo/)

Social Bookmarking and Social Networks

- OnlyWire bookmarking (http://onlywire.com/)

- Hootsuite
  (http://askcharlyleetham.com/recommends/hootsuite/)

Article Marketing

- Ezine Articles (http://ezinearticles.com/)
- Go Articles (http://goarticles.com/)
- Associated Content (http://askcharlyleetham.com/blog/associatedcontent)
- Qondio (http://askcharlyleetham.com/blog/qondio)
- Unique Article Wizard (http://askcharlyleetham.com/blog/uaw)

Content Networks and RSS Feeds

- Hubpages (http://askcharlyleetham.com/blog/hubpages)
- www.feedage.com
- www.feedest.com

Google Analytics

- www.google.com/analytics
- Google Analyticor Plug-In (https://wordpress.org/plugins/google-analyticator/)
- Wordpress Analytics 360 (https://wordpress.org/plugins/analytics360/)

General Resources

- Get Your Blog Online Today
  (http://askcharlyleetham.com/blog/products-services/get-your-blog-online-today)
- www.FreeNetLaw.com

Connect With Charly

If you would like to connect with me, you can via:

http://askcharlyleetham.com/blog/linkedin

https://www.facebook.com/AskCharlyLeetham

http://askcharlyleetham.com/blog/twitter

https://www.google.com/+Askcharlyleetham

The Website Success Accelerator Teaches..

Look out for Other Books in the "Website Success Accelerator Teaches" Series, coming soon

Brought to you by Dreamstone Publishing

http://www.dreamstonepublishing.com

About the Author

Charly Leetham's goal is to assist small business owners realise the power of the Internet as a channel to market their organisations in an appropriate and cost-effective manner. She helps solopreneurs and small businesses map their business processes and plan their web presence.

Charly has a passion for IT and helping people overcome their technology challenges. With more than 24 years experience in the IT industry, ranging from hands-on technical, to high-level business management, Charly has installed and configured computing equipment and has managed business contracts in excess of $26 million dollars.

Charly is familiar with a wide range of web technologies including Wordpress (as a Content Management System, not just a blogging platform); Wishlist Member Plugin to create Membership Sites; Mailchimp and AWeber as Email Service Providers.

Charly believes that businesses should use technology to support their business plan and not, necessarily, drive how business is done. As a result, Charly looks at the best way to integrate different solutions and technologies for the most cost effective way to achieve a businesses objective.

As a result of her endeavours over the last four years, Charly has won the MCEI Women in Business Marketing Award 2010, been shortlisted for the Telstra Business Woman of the Year 2011 awards and awarded Best Entrepreneur – Service Businesses - Up to 100 Employees - Computer Services category in the 8th annual Stevie Awards for Women in Business. Charly was also named in to the Top 100 Women in Ecommerce 2011 and is an honoree for Website Development in the Women In Business Golden Mouse awards.

Qualifications:

Masters of Business Administration (Internet Mktg)

Associate Diploma Electronic Engineering

Other Books from Dreamstone Publishing

Dreamstone publishes books in a wide variety of categories – here are some of our other books:-

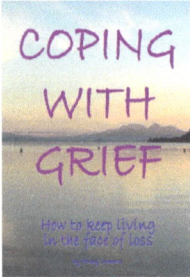

Coping With Grief

By Penny Clements

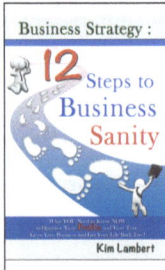

Business Strategy :
12 Steps to Business Sanity
How to Optimize Your Profits and Your Time, Grow Your Business and Get Your Life Back Too!
By Kim Lambert

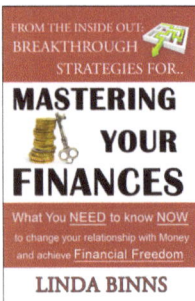

From The Inside Out:
Breakthrough Strategies for Mastering Your Finances:
What YOU Need to Know NOW to Change Your Relationship with Money and Achieve Financial Freedom

By Linda Binns

Look out for further titles in the "How to Bake the Best......" series.

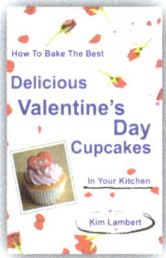

How to Bake the Best Delicious Valentine's Day Cupcakes - In Your Kitchen

By Kim Lambert

How to Bake the Best Delicious Easter Cupcakes and Sweet Treats - In Your Kitchen

By Kim Lambert

(Also available in Spanish)

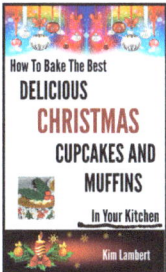

How to Bake the Best Delicious Christmas Cupcakes and Muffins - In Your Kitchen

By Kim Lambert

All Books available from all Amazon sites and other book stores, and available for Kindle too!

www.ingramcontent.com/pod-product-compliance
Lightning Source LLC
Chambersburg PA
CBHW051234090426
42740CB00001B/22